Teacher Created Resources

Listen · Read · Think

SCIENCE

Animals in Danger

Anne Faundez

Teacher Created Resources

First published in the United States by
QEB Publishing, Inc.
23062 La Cadena Drive
Laguna Hills
CA 92653

This edition published by
Teacher Created Resources, Inc.
6421 Industry Way
Westminster, CA 92683

www.teachercreated.com

Library of Congress Catalog Card No. 2004101900

ISBN 1-4206-8148-6

Written by Anne Faundez
Designed by Zeta Jones
Editor Hannah Ray
Picture Researcher Joanne Beardwell

Series Consultant Anne Faundez
Creative Director Louise Morley
Editorial Manager Jean Coppendale

Printed and bound in China

Picture credits

Key: t = top, b = bottom, m = middle, c = center, l =
left, r = right

Corbis/Theo Allofs 18–19, 22cl, /Tom Bean 10, /Tom
Brakefield 6, /Clem Haagner 17, /Martin Harvey
20–21, /Langevin Jacques 5, /Karen Su 4;
Ecoscene/Phillip Colla 14–15; **Getty Images** 7;
Still Pictures/M&C Denis Huot 12–13, /
B Lundberg 8, /C Allan Morgan 16, /H Willcox 9, 22b.

Contents

Under threat

Many types of animal are dying out. These animals are **endangered**.

The animals' homes and food supplies are being destroyed by humans. Humans are also killing large numbers of the animals. This is why the animals become endangered.

In many countries, there are special parks where endangered animals are cared for.

Cheetahs

Cheetahs are the fastest land animals. They live in grassy areas of Africa.

Cheetahs are meat-eaters and eat animals such as hares and antelope.

A baby cheetah is called a cub.

Cubs are gray with long wooly hair along their backs.

Cheetah cubs stay with their mother for about a year.

Cheetahs live for about ten to twelve years in the wild.

Hazel dormice

Hazel dormice live in Great Britain. They are a type of mouse.

They have big, sharp front teeth and long, furry tails.

8

Hazel dormice sleep, or **hibernate**, in winter. They are also **nocturnal**. This means that they are awake at night and sleep during the day.

Whooping cranes

Whooping cranes have long beaks and long legs. The adult bird is snowy white with a black tip on each wing.

Whooping cranes are the tallest birds in North America. They travel in groups, or **flocks**.

They make a "whoop" sound when in danger. That is why they are called whooping cranes.

African elephants

The African elephant is the world's largest land **mammal**.

Elephants live in a family group, led by an older female.

Elephants eat grass, leaves, and bark. They use their tusks for peeling bark off trees, digging and looking for roots.

They live for up to seventy years.

Blue whales

Blue whales are mammals that live in the sea.

The blue whale is the biggest animal in the world. It measures about 100 feet long.

Blue whales eat large amounts of small, shrimp-like animals called krill.

Blue whales have baleen plates instead of teeth. These plates trap the krill but let the water out again.

Blue whales live for about eighty years.

Leatherback turtles

Leatherback turtles are the largest living **reptiles**. They can grow up to eight feet long. They have a leathery shell and flippers that do not have claws.

Leatherbacks always return to the same beach to lay their eggs. When they have hatched from their eggs, the babies find their own way to the sea.

Yellow-footed rock wallabies

Yellow-footed rock wallabies belong to the kangaroo family.

Wallabies and kangaroos have very strong back legs and hop along the ground, using their tails to balance.

Yellow-footed rock wallabies live in steep and rocky areas of Australia. Their fur matches the color of the rocks. This is called **camouflage** and makes it very difficult for **predators** to see the wallabies.

Mountain gorillas

Mountain gorillas are the largest type of gorilla. They live in the forests of some African countries.

Mountain gorillas live in groups. The adult male is called a silverback.

The silverback beats his chest to warn the others of danger.

Mountain gorillas' favorite food is bamboo shoots.

Mountain gorillas can live for up to fifty years.

Glossary

camouflage—something that makes an animal look part of its surroundings.

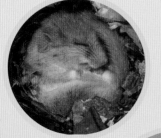

endangered—an animal that is in danger of dying out.

flock—a group of birds.

hibernate—to sleep through the winter until the weather warms up.

mammal—an animal that feeds on its mother's milk.

22

nocturnal—an animal that is active at night, rather than during the day.

predator—an animal that hunts, kills, and eats other animals for food.

reptile—a cold-blooded animal, such as a snake or a lizard. Often covered in scales.

Index

Parents' and teachers' notes

- Ask your child questions about the picture on the front cover of the book. What does he/she think the book is about? Read the title to your child. Does he/she still think their original guess about the subject of the book is correct?
- Look through the book. Ask your child to choose his/her favorite picture and read that page first. Explain that the pages do not have to be read in order, as they would in a storybook.
- Look at the contents page, the glossary, and the index. Explain that these are often found in books that give information (i.e. nonfiction).
- Tell your child that an index helps us find out where to locate certain information in a book. Look at the order of the words in the index (alphabetical). Sing an alphabet song to remind your child of alphabetical order.
- Point out the words that are in **bold** type. Explain that they are unusual or difficult words and that the glossary helps us understand what they mean.
- Together, read about the leatherback turtle. Draw around a dinner plate and ask your child to add a head, tail, and flippers to the "shell" and to color it in. Label your child's picture, asking him/her to help you by suggesting what needs to be labeled.
- Read about the cheetah. Where does it live?
- Use a globe or an atlas to find a map of Africa.
- Which other animals in the book live in Africa?
- Can your child remember how the whooping crane got its name? Can he/she make a "whooping" noise?
- Can your child jump like a yellow-footed rock wallaby? Can your child beat his/her chest, just like the silverback gorilla?
- Make a collage of your child's favorite endangered animal using photographs from old magazines, paint, crayons, scraps of fabric, and other materials.